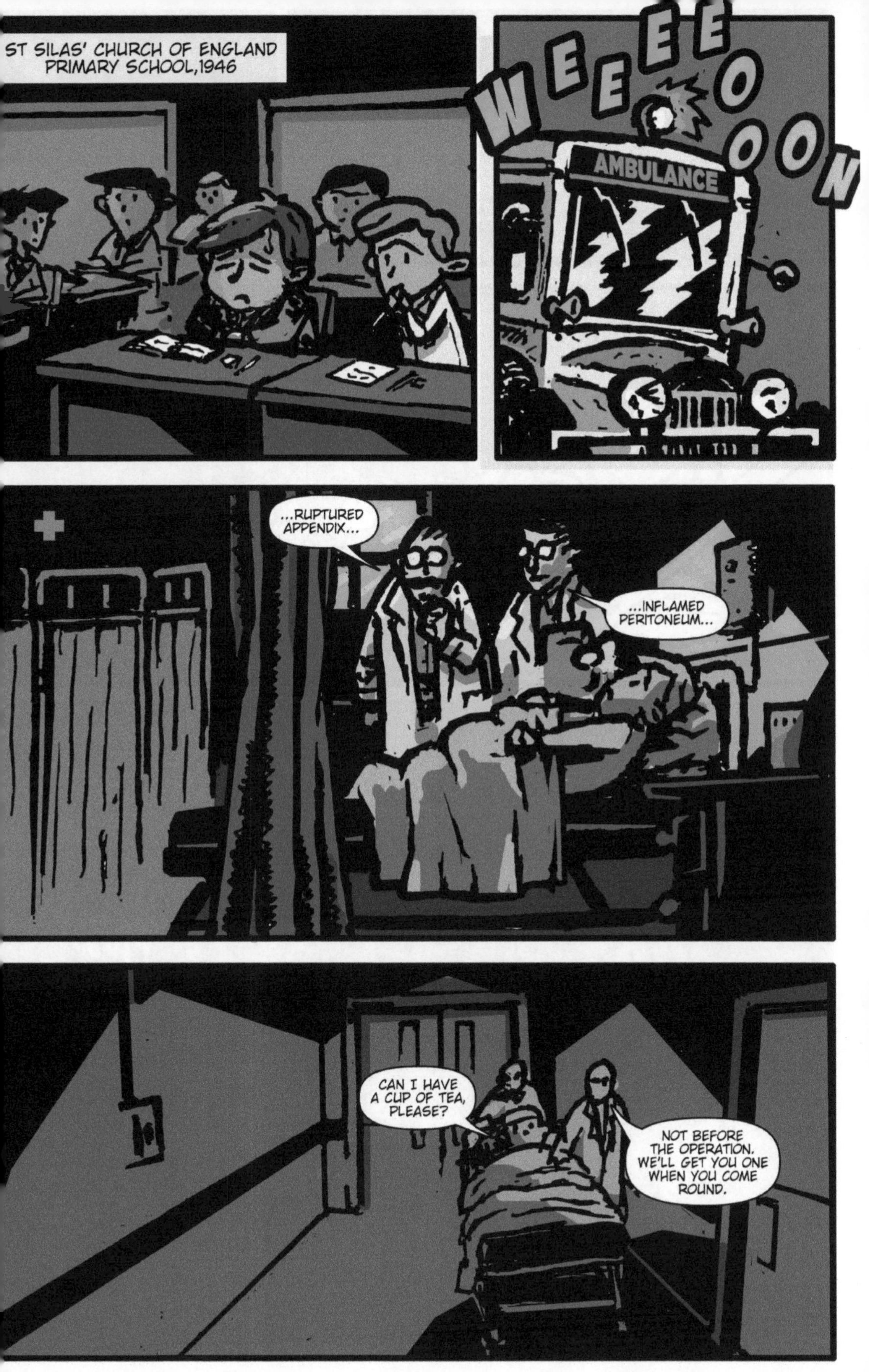
ST SILAS' CHURCH OF ENGLAND PRIMARY SCHOOL, 1946
WEEEEOOON
AMBULANCE
...RUPTURED APPENDIX...
...INFLAMED PERITONEUM...
CAN I HAVE A CUP OF TEA, PLEASE?
NOT BEFORE THE OPERATION. WE'LL GET YOU ONE WHEN YOU COME ROUND.

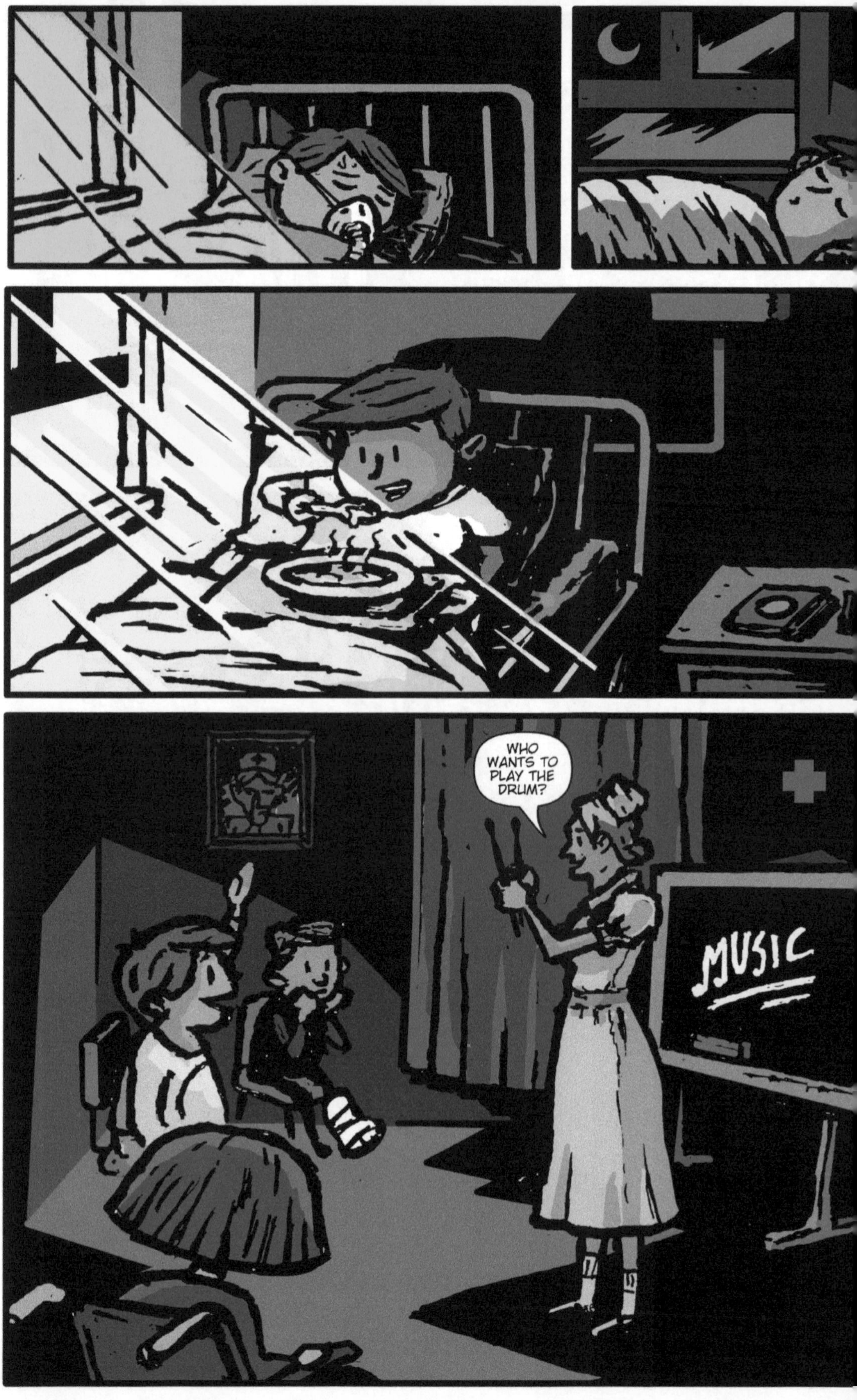
WHO WANTS TO PLAY THE DRUM?
MUSIC

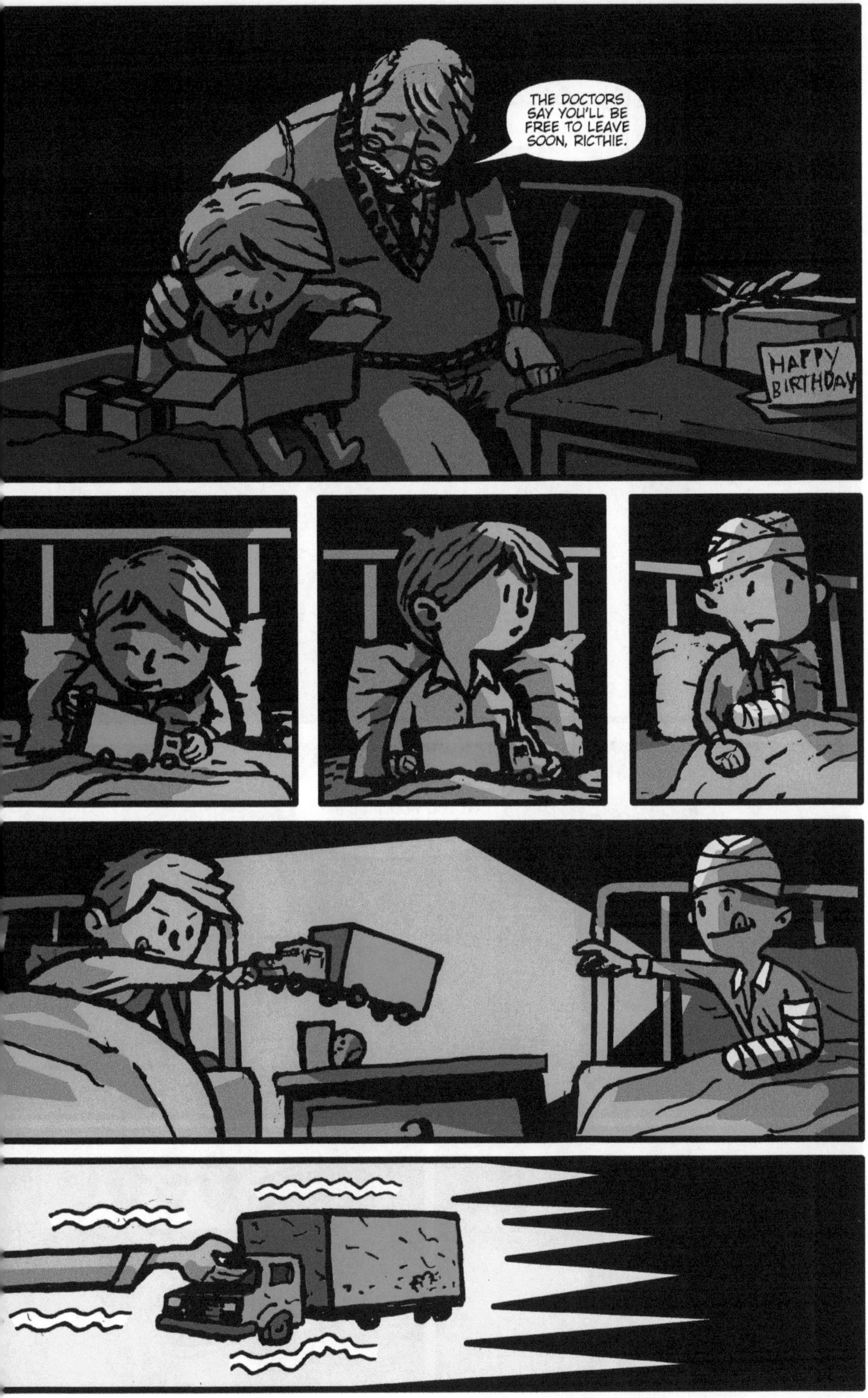
THE DOCTORS SAY YOU'LL BE FREE TO LEAVE SOON, RICTHIE.
HAPPY BIRTHDAY

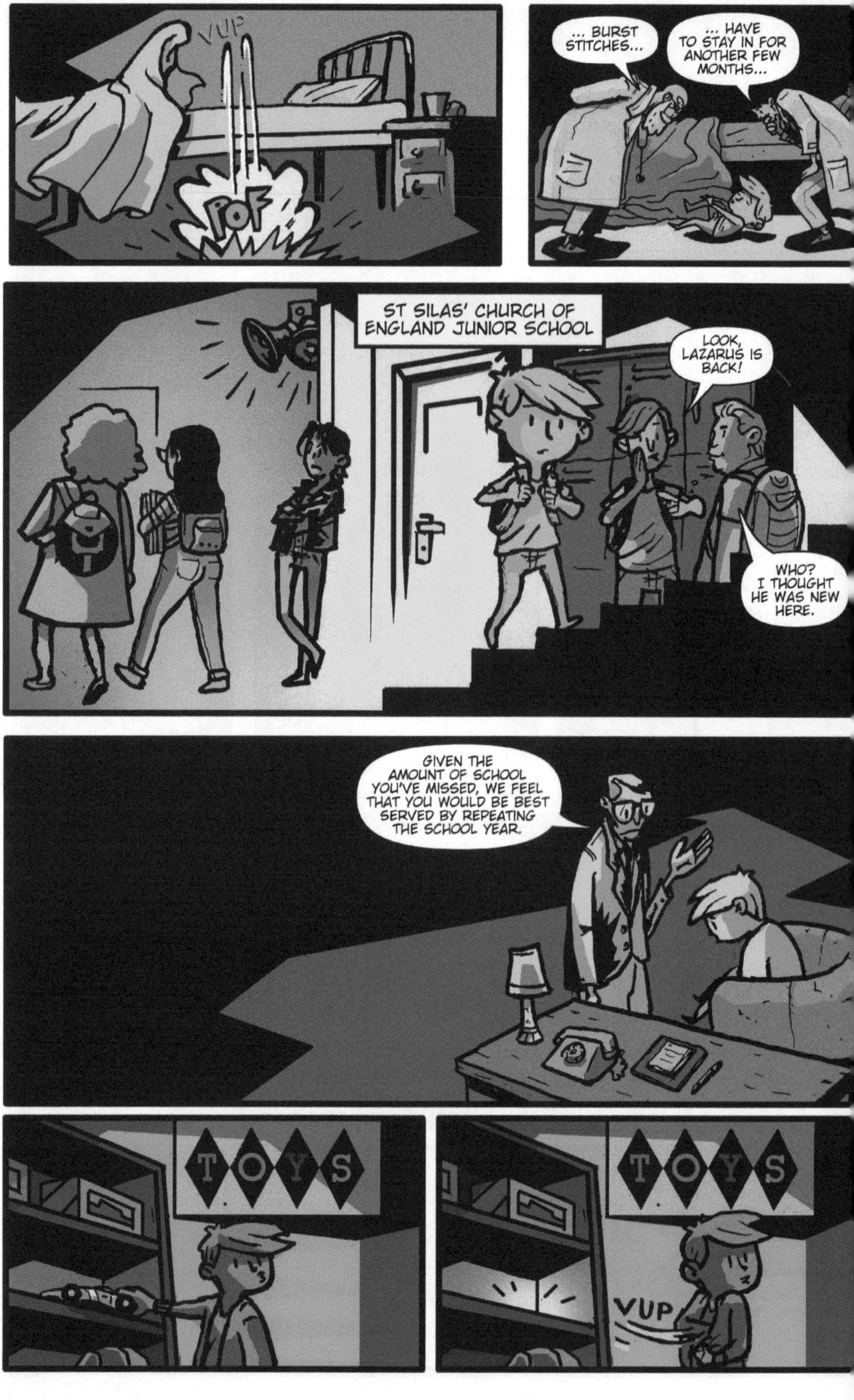
VUP
POF
... BURST STITCHES...
... HAVE TO STAY IN FOR ANOTHER FEW MONTHS...
ST SILAS' CHURCH OF ENGLAND JUNIOR SCHOOL
LOOK, LAZARUS IS BACK!
WHO? I THOUGHT HE WAS NEW HERE.
GIVEN THE AMOUNT OF SCHOOL YOU'VE MISSED, WE FEEL THAT YOU WOULD BE BEST SERVED BY REPEATING THE SCHOOL YEAR.
TOYS
TOYS
VUP

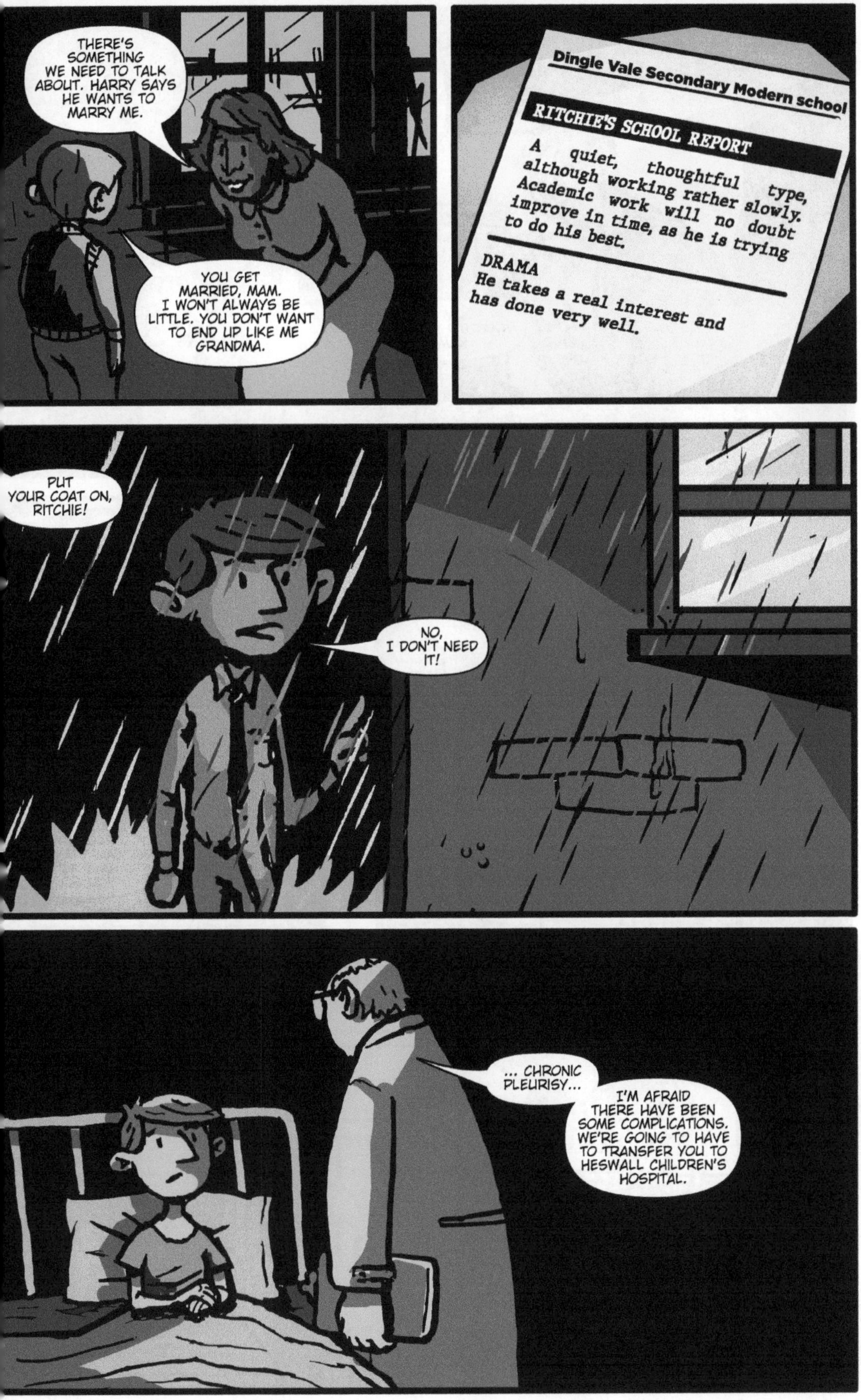
THERE'S SOMETHING WE NEED TO TALK ABOUT. HARRY SAYS HE WANTS TO MARRY ME.
YOU GET MARRIED, MAM. I WON'T ALWAYS BE LITTLE. YOU DON'T WANT TO END UP LIKE ME GRANDMA.
Dingle Vale Secondary Modern school
RITCHIE'S SCHOOL REPORT
A quiet, thoughtful type, although working rather slowly. Academic work will no doubt improve in time, as he is trying to do his best.
DRAMA
He takes a real interest and has done very well.
PUT YOUR COAT ON, RITCHIE!
NO, I DON'T NEED IT!
... CHRONIC PLEURISY...
I'M AFRAID THERE HAVE BEEN SOME COMPLICATIONS. WE'RE GOING TO HAVE TO TRANSFER YOU TO HESWALL CHILDREN'S HOSPITAL.

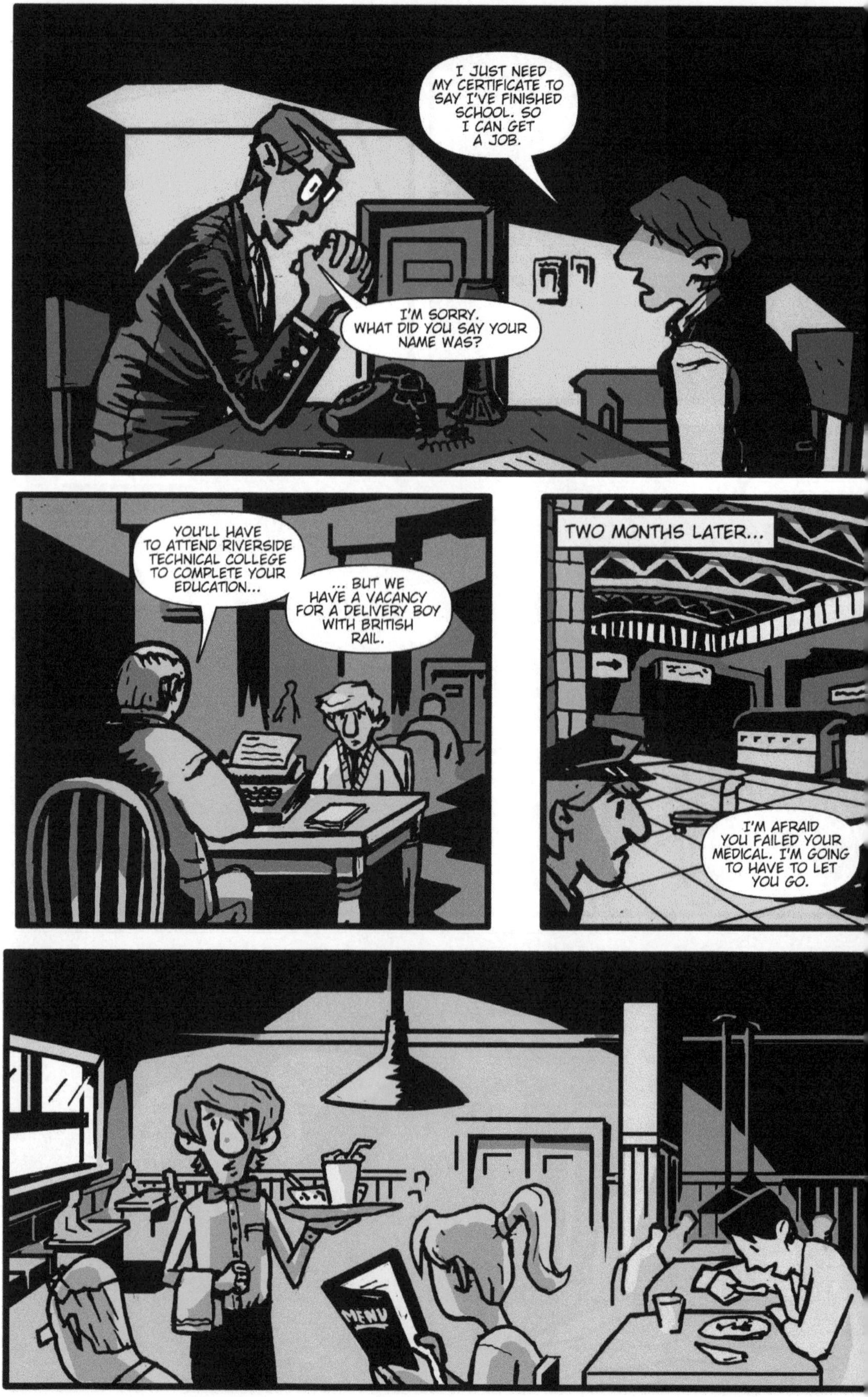
I JUST NEED MY CERTIFICATE TO SAY I'VE FINISHED SCHOOL. SO I CAN GET A JOB.
I'M SORRY. WHAT DID YOU SAY YOUR NAME WAS?
YOU'LL HAVE TO ATTEND RIVERSIDE TECHNICAL COLLEGE TO COMPLETE YOUR EDUCATION...
... BUT WE HAVE A VACANCY FOR A DELIVERY BOY WITH BRITISH RAIL.
TWO MONTHS LATER...
I'M AFRAID YOU FAILED YOUR MEDICAL. I'M GOING TO HAVE TO LET YOU GO.
MENU

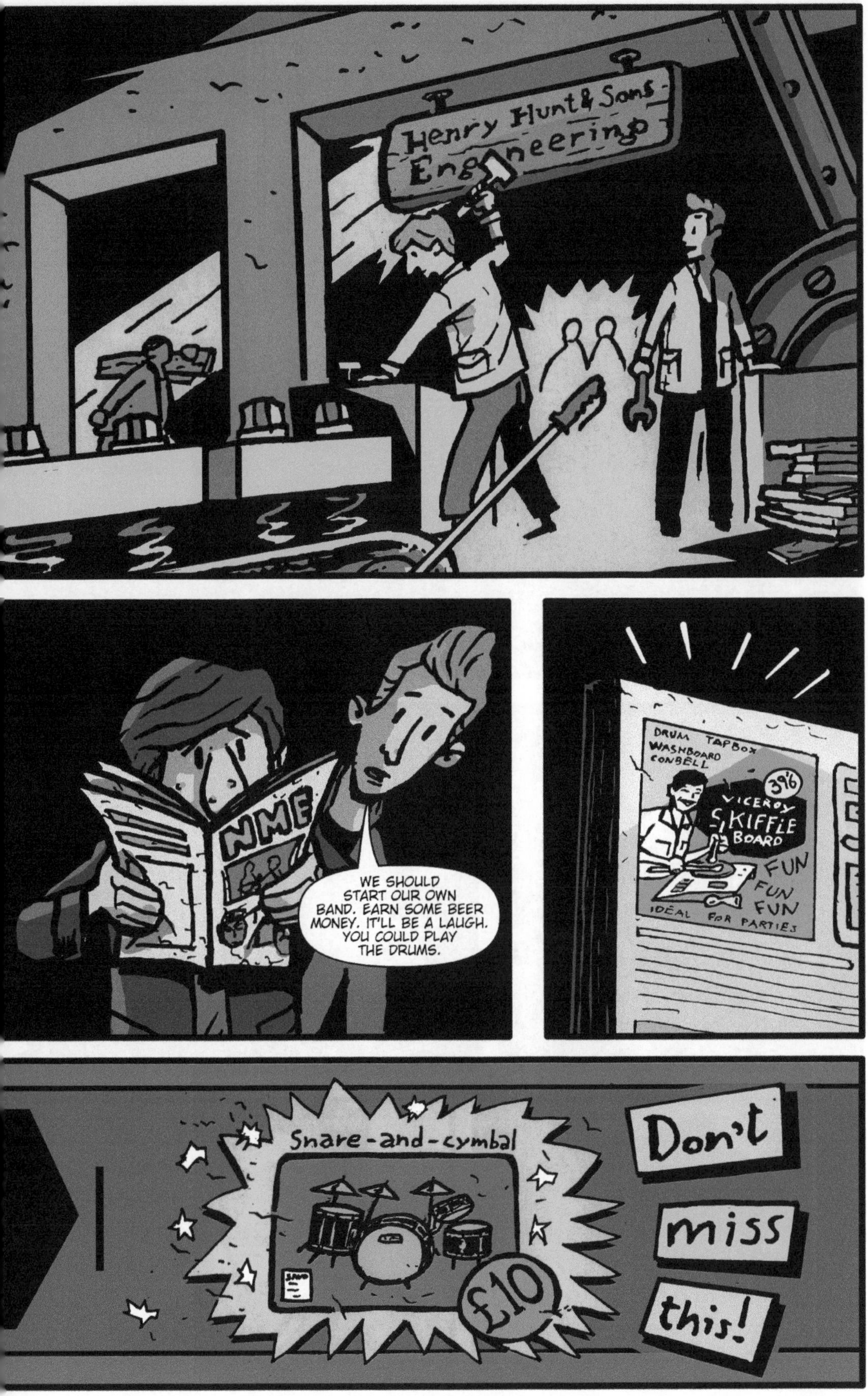
Henry Hunt & Sons Engineering
NME
WE SHOULD START OUR OWN BAND. EARN SOME BEER MONEY. IT'LL BE A LAUGH. YOU COULD PLAY THE DRUMS.
DRUM TAPBOX WASHBOARD CONBELL
VICEROY SKIFFLE BOARD
FUN FUN FUN
IDEAL FOR PARTIES
Snare-and-cymbal
£10
Don't miss this!

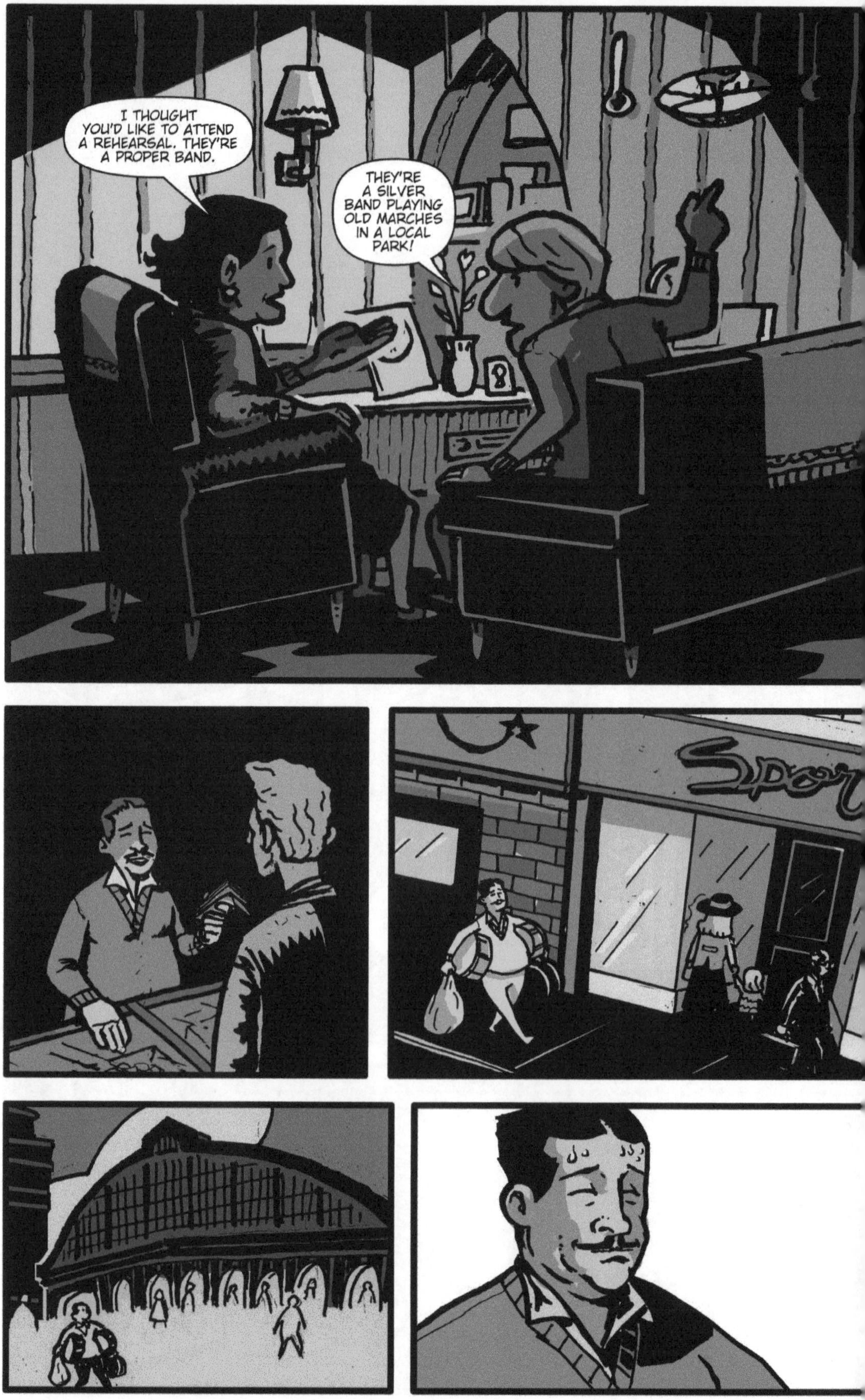
I THOUGHT YOU'D LIKE TO ATTEND A REHEARSAL. THEY'RE A PROPER BAND.
THEY'RE A SILVER BAND PLAYING OLD MARCHES IN A LOCAL PARK!
Spor

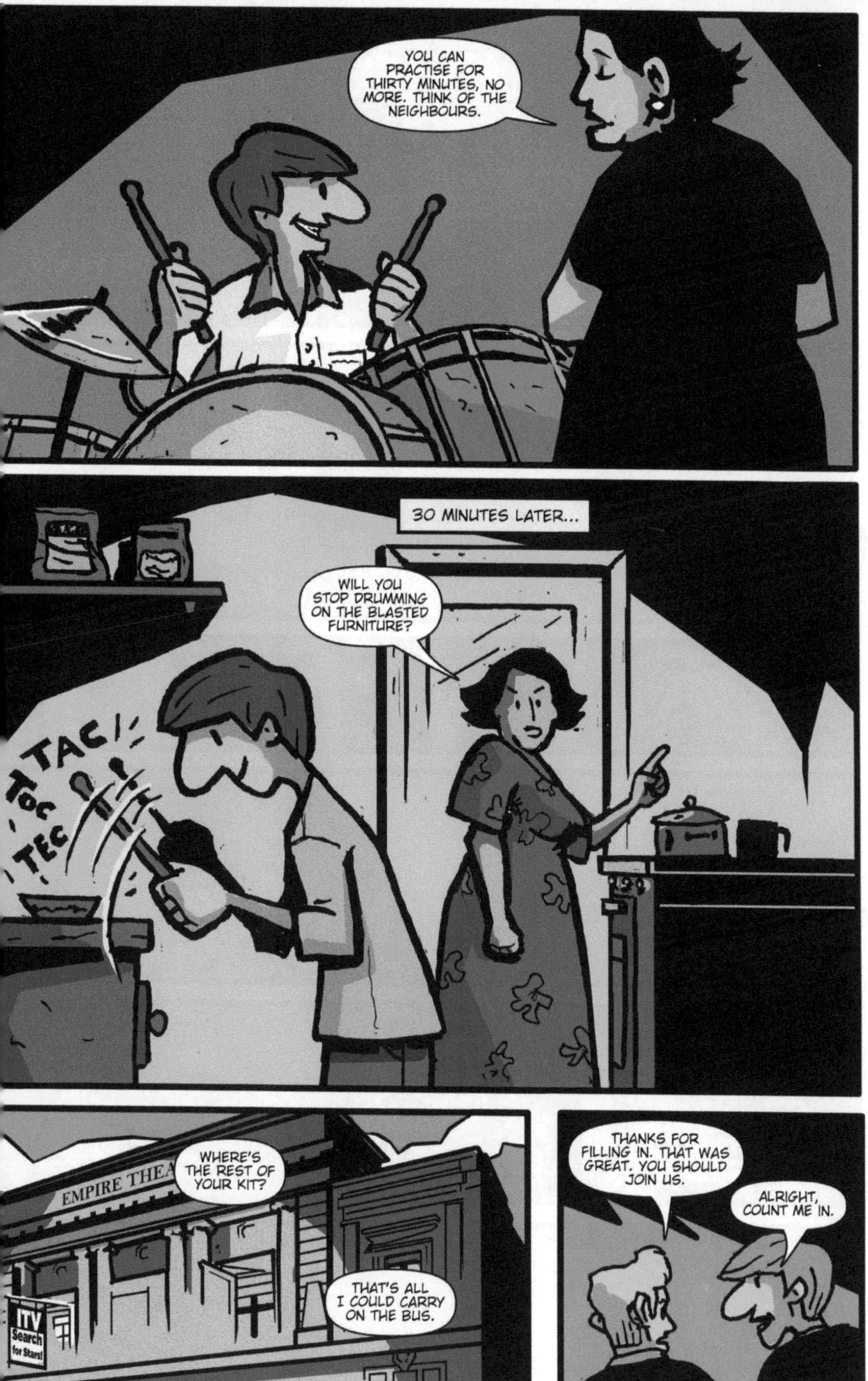

YOU CAN PRACTISE FOR THIRTY MINUTES, NO MORE. THINK OF THE NEIGHBOURS.
30 MINUTES LATER...
WILL YOU STOP DRUMMING ON THE BLASTED FURNITURE?
TAC
TOC
TEC
EMPIRE THEA
ITV Search for Stars!
WHERE'S THE REST OF YOUR KIT?
THAT'S ALL I COULD CARRY ON THE BUS.
THANKS FOR FILLING IN. THAT WAS GREAT. YOU SHOULD JOIN US.
ALRIGHT, COUNT ME IN.

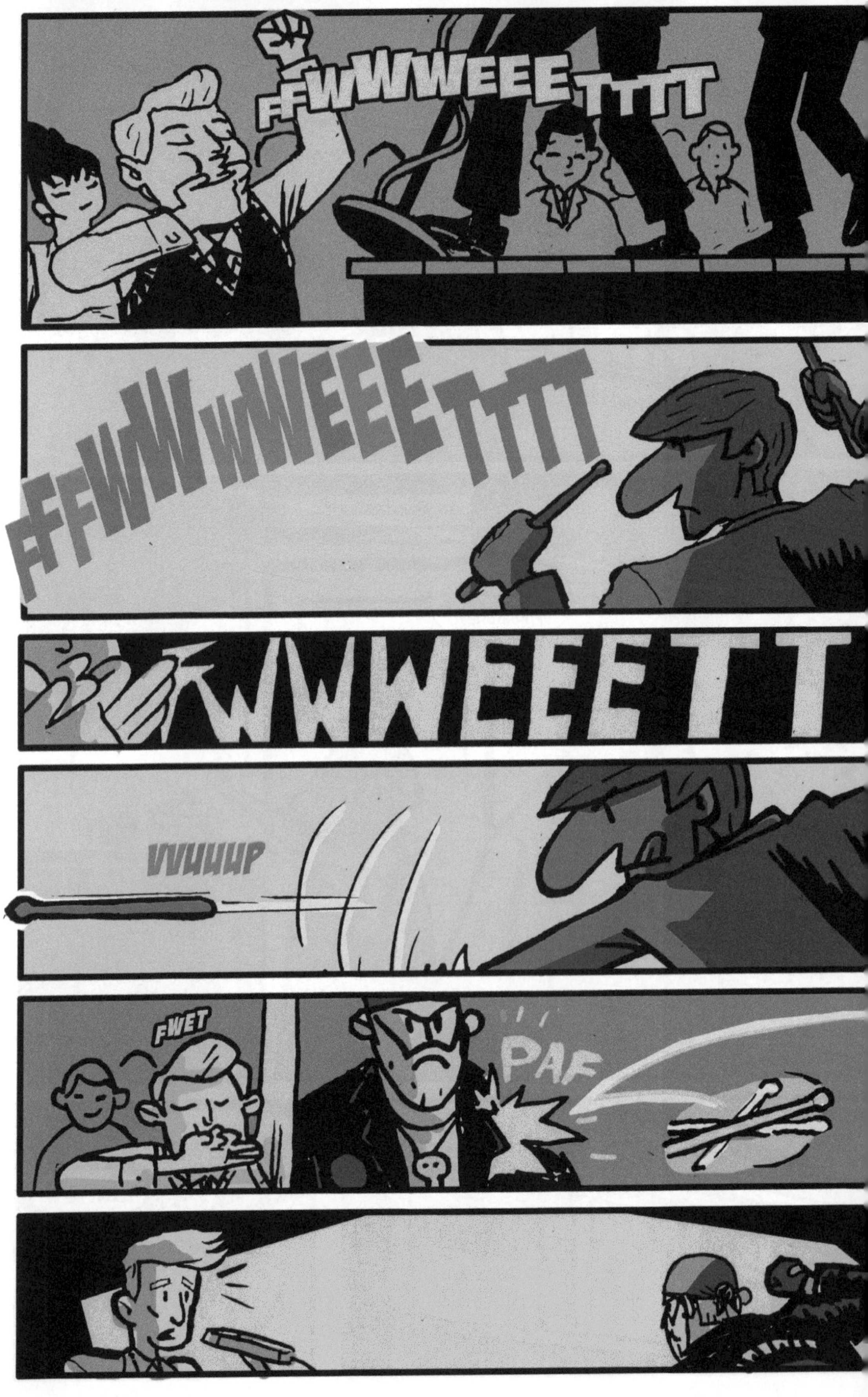
FFWWWEEETTTT
FFWWWWWEEETTTT
WWWEEETT
VVUUUP
FWET
PAF

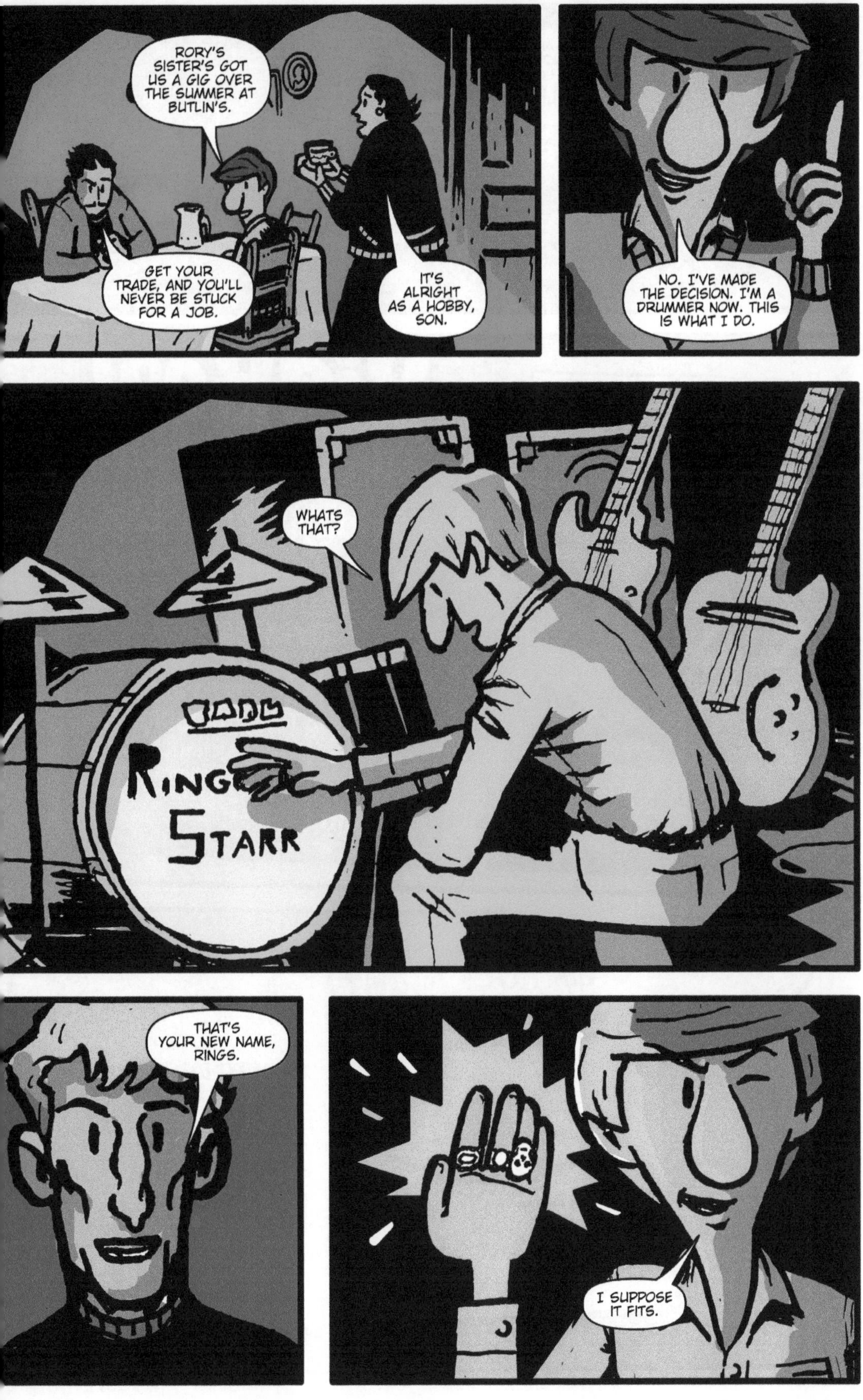
RORY'S SISTER'S GOT US A GIG OVER THE SUMMER AT BUTLIN'S.
GET YOUR TRADE, AND YOU'LL NEVER BE STUCK FOR A JOB.
IT'S ALRIGHT AS A HOBBY, SON.
NO. I'VE MADE THE DECISION. I'M A DRUMMER NOW. THIS IS WHAT I DO.
WHATS THAT?
RINGO STARR
THAT'S YOUR NEW NAME, RINGS.
I SUPPOSE IT FITS.

CAN I GET AN AUTOGRAPH?

I BET YOU WON'T GO AND KISS PAUL.

JUST BECAUSE YOU'RE SCARED TO DO IT.

YOU'RE SCARED, MAUREEN!

OKAY, FINE.

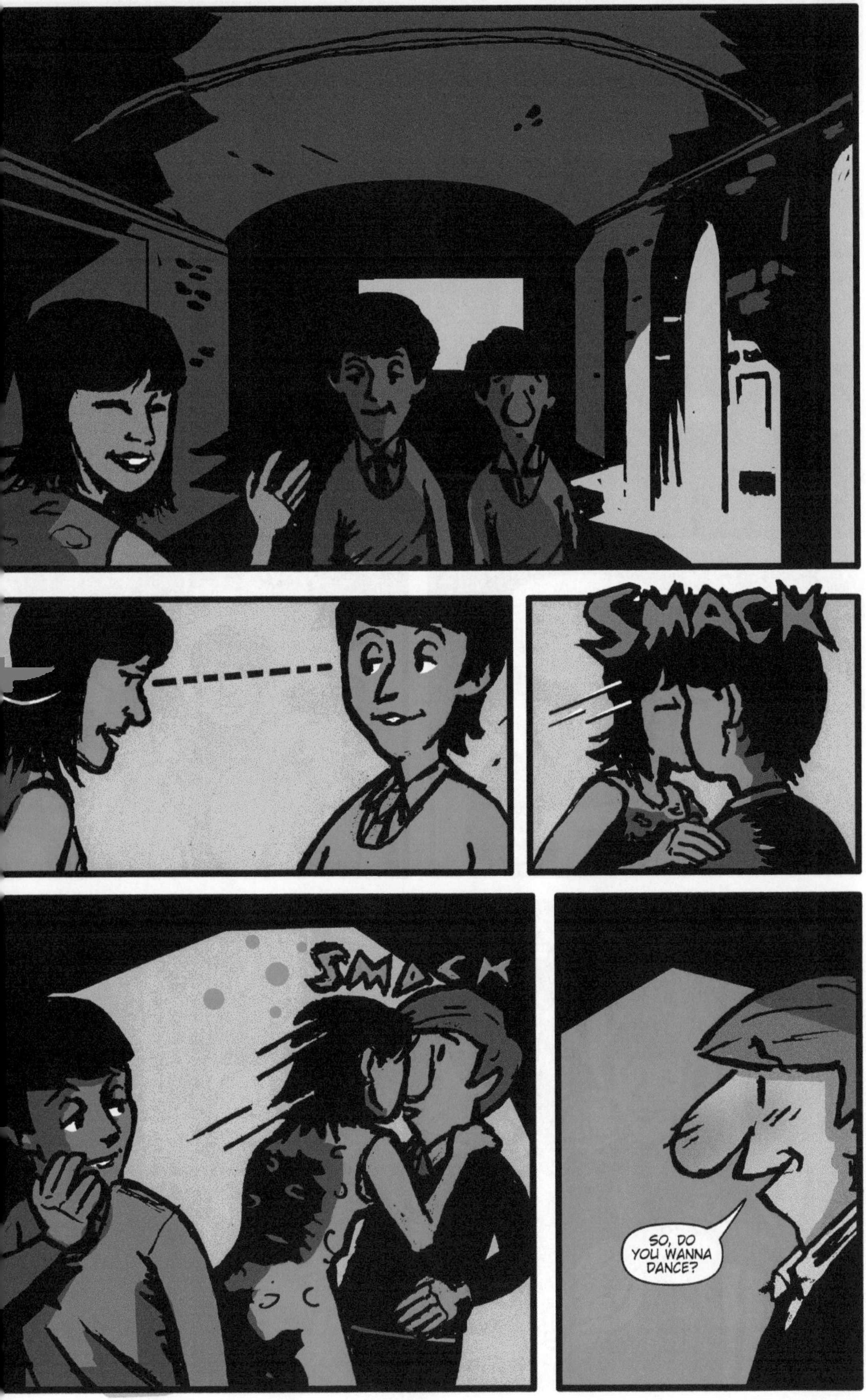
SMACK
SMACK
SO, DO YOU WANNA DANCE?

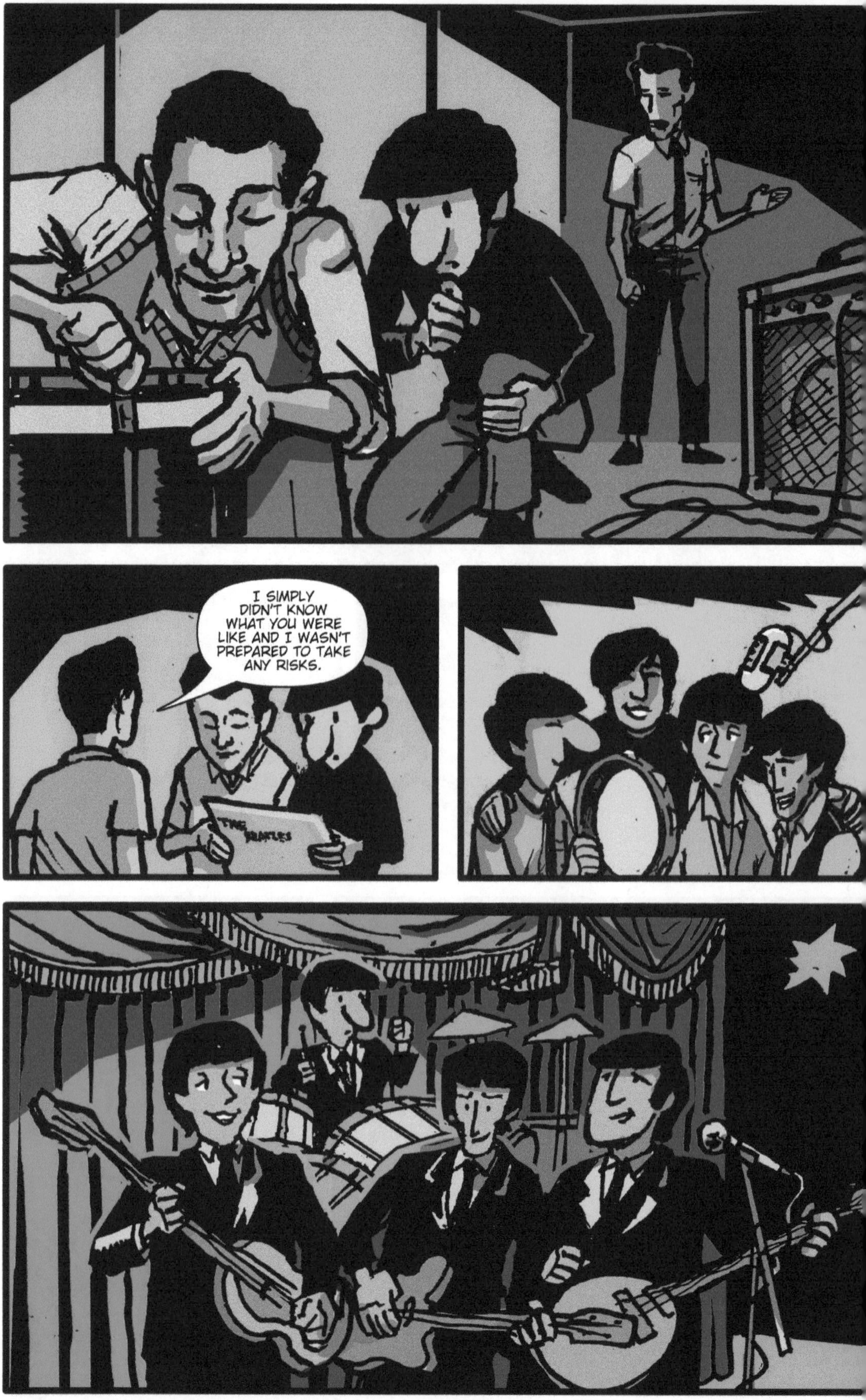
I SIMPLY DIDN'T KNOW WHAT YOU WERE LIKE AND I WASN'T PREPARED TO TAKE ANY RISKS.
THE BEATLES

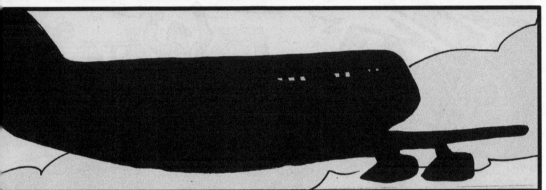

"IT TOOK ABOUT TWO YEARS TO GET EACH OTHER SORTED OUT, BUT FROM THEN ON I HAD THE FEELING THERE WAS FOUR OF US IN IT. I SUPPOSE WE GOT ON TOGETHER BECAUSE WE'RE THE ONLY FOUR PEOPLE LIKE US; WE'RE THE ONLY ONES WHO REALLY KNOW WHAT IT'S LIKE. WHEN THERE WAS ALL THAT BEATLEMANIA WE WERE PUSHED INTO A CORNER, JUST THE FOUR OF US. A SORT OF TRAP, REALLY. WE WERE LIKE SIAMESE QUADS, EATING OUT OF THE SAME BOWL."

TIDALWAVE
COMICS

David Cromarty — Writer

Victor Moura — Pencils

Benjamin Glibert — Letters

Victor Moura — Colors

Graham Hill — Cover

Darren G. Davis
Publisher

Maggie Jessup
Publicity

Susan Ferris
Entertainment Manager

Steven Diggs Jr.
Marketing Manager

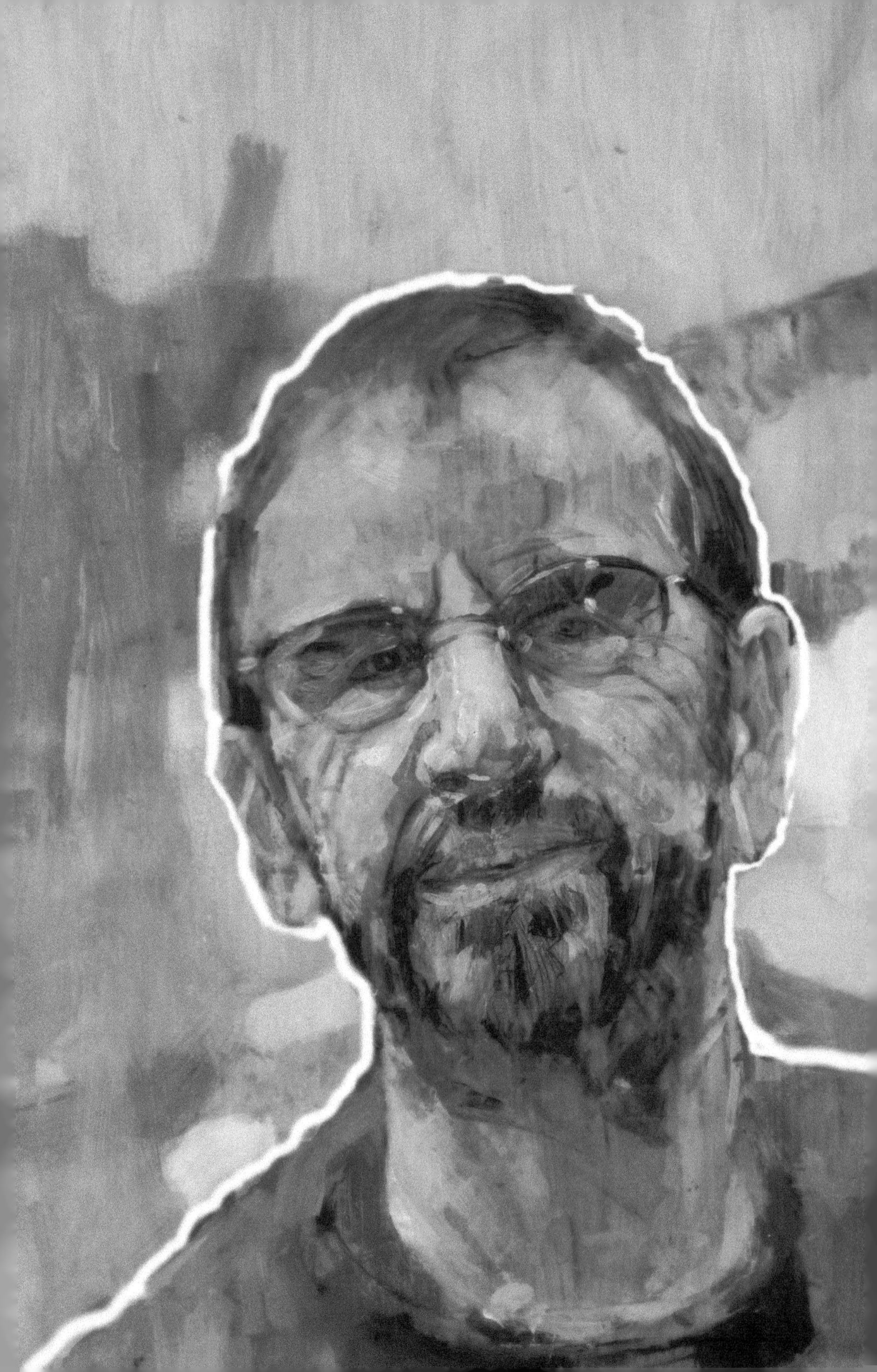

Lightning Source UK Ltd.
Milton Keynes UK
UKHW051057140122
397133UK00002B/24

9 781956 841954